B. THE EQUATORIAL FORESTS OF
AFRICA, ASIA AND AUSTRALIA

NEW VISUAL GEOGRAPHY

The Equatorial Forests

NEW VISUAL GEOGRAPHY

W. G. Moore

Regional

ICE-CAP AND TUNDRA
THE NORTHERN FORESTS
THE TEMPERATE GRASSLANDS
DESERTS OF THE WORLD
THE TROPICAL GRASSLANDS
THE EQUATORIAL FORESTS
THE MEDITERRANEAN LANDS
THE MONSOON LANDS

Economic

THE MINING OF COAL
IRON AND STEEL PRODUCTION
THE PRODUCTION OF OIL

Physical

RIVERS AND THEIR WORK
THE SEA AND THE COAST
THE WEATHER
MOUNTAINS AND PLATEAUX

NEW VISUAL GEOGRAPHY

Regional Series

The Equatorial Forests

W. G. MOORE

HUTCHINSON EDUCATIONAL

HUTCHINSON EDUCATIONAL LTD
178–202 Great Portland Street, London W1

London Melbourne Sydney
Auckland Johannesburg Cape Town
and agencies throughout the world

First published July 1969
Second impression March 1971

This book has been set in Baskerville type, printed in Great Britain
on coated paper by Anchor Press, and
bound by Wm. Brendon, both of Tiptree, Essex

ISBN 0 09 096840 9 (cased)
0 09 096841 7 (paperback)

Contents

The end-papers were drawn by
DENYS BAKER

Acknowledgement is due to the following for permission to reproduce photographs: E. Aubert de la Rue, Nos. 3, 4, 5, 6; Jack Barker, by courtesy of United Africa Co. Ltd., Nos. 8, 16; Cadbury Bros. Ltd., No. 23; Camera Press Ltd., Nos. 11, 25, 26; J. Allan Cash, Nos. 1, 15; Central Office of Information, Nos. 12, 13; Conselho Nacional de Geografia, Brazil, No. 2; Elders and Fyffes, Ltd., No. 24; F.A.O. No. 28; Ghana Information Services, Accra, No. 14; Natural Rubber Producers' Research Association, Nos. 19, 20, 21; Press Association Ltd., No. 9; Radio Times Hulton Picture Library, No. 10; Shell International Petroleum Co. Ltd., Nos. 7, 22, 27; Unilever Ltd., Nos. 17, 18.

Facts and Figures

Climate The figures below show that temperatures are always high and rainfall is heavy and well distributed throughout the year. There are no real seasons: the weather is hot and humid all the time. Find all the places in your atlas.

	Average temp. hottest month	Average temp. coldest month	Mean annual rainfall
South America			
Manáus	28°C	27°C	70 in.
Belém	27°C	25°C	90 in.
Africa			
Yaoundé	23°C	21°C	62 in.
Nouvelle Anvers	27°C	24°C	67 in.
Asia			
Singapore	27°C	26°C	95 in.
Sandakan	28°C	27°C	120 in.

Products All the countries below have large equatorial forest regions and are mentioned in this book. The list gives the output of rubber, cocoa, and palm oil and kernels (in thousand tons), which are products of the equatorial forest region, in some of these countries.

	Rubber	*Cocoa*	*Palm oil and kernels*
Brazil	28	123	
Malaya	825		126
Nigeria	71	220	420
Ghana		450	
Congo (Kinshasa)			305
Indonesia	683		160

PART ONE: THE LANDS AND THE PEOPLES

1 West African rain forest: near Wiawso in south-west Ghana

The equatorial forests or tropical rain forests of Africa occupy much of the basin of the River Congo, and extend in a belt of varying width along the coast of the Gulf of Guinea (*see* endpaper map B). In the Malagasy Republic (Madagascar) they cover a strip of land along the east coast. The picture shows a section of the equatorial forest in south-west Ghana, near the village of Wiawso. This part of the country has an annual rainfall of 60 to 90 inches and is almost entirely covered with forest. Do you see the hills in the distance? The rainfall is heavier and the forest is denser on the windward slopes of these hills—slopes which face the dominant moisture-laden winds from the sea. As you look over the forest, you are probably first struck by its luxuriant growth. A great expanse of green foliage stretches to the horizon, and nowhere can you see the ground.

Notice that the trees are not all of the same height. Here and there single trees reach a height of up to 200 feet, towering above all the others. There are two trees like this on the right and left of the picture, in the foreground. Their trunks are straight and have small crowns and no lower branches. Beneath these very tall trees is a vast number of others which reach a height of about 120 feet and form an almost closed canopy over the forest. Below these trees is another layer at about half their height: trees with low branches and heavier crowns. At ground level, in spots where the sunlight penetrates the foliage, grasses, shrubs and other low plants are growing. In the equatorial climate there is no cold or dry season, so that the trees and other plants go on growing all through the year. Most of the trees are evergreen but along with them are a few *deciduous* species—trees that shed their leaves every year. But the deciduous species do not all shed their leaves at the same time, so the forest as a whole always *looks* green. The numbers of deciduous trees increase towards the edge of the equatorial forest, where there is a marked dry season and where forest gradually passes into savanna or tropical grassland.

ANSWER THESE QUESTIONS

1 How many different 'layers' of trees are there in the West African rain forest? What are the approximate heights of the trees in these layers?

2 Why does the tropical rain forest always look green?

2 *South American rain forest: in the Amazon valley, Brazil*

A second great area of equatorial forest is in Central and South America. By far the greater part lies in the basin of the River Amazon, in Brazil, and this forest is known by the Portuguese name *selva*, or in the plural *selvas*: words which are also sometimes used for equatorial forests in other areas of the world. As in Central Africa, the abundant rainfall which helps to maintain a luxuriant forest growth also feeds a mighty river. The picture shows a short stretch of the Amazon as well as a small section of the *selva* which extends across its basin. Can you see any evidence of human settlement? The *selva* has probably been less changed by man than any other major region of natural vegetation in the world, and it has been well called 'a great plant museum'.

Along much of its course the Amazon has no definite banks separating it from the forest: the picture illustrates why this is so. You can see (foreground) how the river has flooded part of the nearby forest, so that the trees are standing in water. Each year the heavy tropical rain combines with the melting snows from the Andes to send a gigantic surge of water into the main stream. The river is at its highest about June, when it floods thousands of square miles of the *selva*. Only trees which can stand having their roots in water for weeks or even months at a time are able to survive. This means that on the flood-plain of the Amazon and its tributaries, known in Brazil as the *várzea*, the type of forest differs from that on the higher ground which the floods do not reach (*see* No. 3). The forest is denser and more varied (bottom left). Yet here there are patches of grassland (centre left), sometimes so extensive that cattle ranching is important, e.g. on Marajó island at the mouth of the Amazon.

Notice how the river has deposited silt on the inside of the great curve in the picture, creating new islands. On the opposite side it is cutting into the banks and pushing back the forest. Sometimes the river undermines its banks over a long distance, and soil, trees, and a tangled mass of vegetation crash into the water and are carried downstream.

ANSWER THESE QUESTIONS

1 What are the Brazilian (Portuguese) names for (a) the equatorial forests of the Amazon basin, (b) the flood-plain of the Amazon and its tributaries?

2 Why does the type of forest on the flood-plain of the Amazon differ from that on the higher ground?

3 *In the Amazon forest: near the Tumuc Humac Mountains, Brazil*

In the previous pictures you saw the equatorial forest from a distance. This picture shows the interior of the forest: it was taken near the Tumuc Humac Mountains, in Amapá State. The forest here stands on the high ground or *terra firme* above the Amazon flood-plain. Dense as it is, the forest on the *terra firme* is more open than the forest of the *várzea* (No. 2). Notice how much sunlight is penetrating the canopy: the denser parts of the *várzea* forest are gloomy, silent and dank under the almost closed canopy of trees, and there is little undergrowth.

From the air the forest looks like a uniform green carpet (No. 2), but, as the picture shows, it really consists of an immense number of different plants. There may be as many as three thousand species in a square mile of forest. There are no large stands of a single kind of tree, as there are in the coniferous forests of higher latitudes (*see The Northern Forests*). You can check this by simply counting the different kinds of leaves that you can see in the picture. The leaves of these trees and other plants in the equatorial forests are mostly large, leathery and dark green. Their smooth upper surfaces help them to shed the heavy tropical rain, so that *transpiration* (loss of water vapour) is not prevented for too long. Now look at the trunks of those trees that are clearly visible in the sunlight: they are straight, slender, and have no lower branches. Like most of the trees of the rain forest, they have smooth, thin barks, for they need no protection from the cold. Notice how similar they are to the tall trees in the foreground of No. 1. The great majority of the trees here, as in the tropical rain forests of Africa, are evergreen, and there are relatively few *deciduous* species.

In its animal life the Amazon rain forest is much poorer than the African. It has not many animals that live at ground level: most of them, like the monkeys, are tree dwellers. But, as you might expect, there is rich bird life high up in the trees, including the brilliantly coloured parrots, and a vast number of insects, including many beautiful butterflies and moths.

ANSWER THESE QUESTIONS

1 Which type of forest has the greater number of species per square mile—the equatorial forest or the northern coniferous forest?

2 How would you describe the trees of the equatorial forest with regard to (a) their leaves, (b) their trunks, and (c) their bark?

4 Climbing plants: lians in the Araguari valley, Brazil

The woody climbing plants known as *lianes* or *lianas*, sometimes called *vines*, are among the most remarkable features of the equatorial forest. They have their roots in the soil, but they cannot grow far upwards without support. There are hundreds of species of liane, and they occur in all the main equatorial forest regions, but the largest collection is in the selva of South America.

The picture, showing some typical lianes, was taken in the valley of the Araguari river, in Amapá State, Brazil. Notice the number of different lianes clinging to the trunk of the large tree. As you see, some lianes are as thin as cords, others are thicker than a man's arm. Wherever a liane happens to be in the forest, it will continue to grow until it finds a tree to support it. Once it has found one, it usually grows quickly up this tree until it reaches the light at the top. Often it does not give off any branches until it has grown to that level. Then it may pass to a neighbouring tree, and possibly another, continuing its growth high up in the forest canopy. If a tree is cut through near ground level, it may be held upright by the lianes that are attached to it. Sometimes the liane ascends one tree to the top, crosses over, and descends another. Some species such as the *rattan*, a climbing palm which is common in the equatorial forests of Indonesia and Malaya, reach a length of 500 feet or more. There is also a small number of shorter lianes which do not rise far above the ground and never reach the forest canopy.

Lianes attach themselves to their supports in different ways. One type winds itself round and round the tree as it grows: the dappled liane on the right of the tree in the picture is of this kind. Another type holds on by means of special roots, another by tendrils, and another by hooked thorns. Can you recognise any of these in the picture? In the struggle for light and space in the equatorial forest all these lianes are in competition with the trees. If the trees are of value to man, the lianes can only be looked upon as weeds to be cut down.

ANSWER THESE QUESTIONS

1 On which side of the River Amazon, north or south, does Amapá State lie? (Use your atlas.)

2 In what different ways do lianes attach themselves to their supports?

5 *Lianes and epiphytes: in the Maroni valley, French Guiana*

This picture was taken in the tropical rain forest of the upper Maroni valley in French Guiana. In the foreground is a long thick *liane*, hanging down from the forest canopy. This sometimes happens because the liane becomes too heavy for its supporting branch, which breaks, causing it to fall. An equally interesting feature in the picture is the group plants attached to the liane (left). These are ferns which are actually growing on the liane, well above the water and the forest floor. They are known as *epiphytes*. Perhaps you noticed one on the trunk of the large tree in No. 4. Epiphytes occupy an important place in the rich vegetation of the equatorial forest. They occur in the three major regions of equatorial forest, and are most numerous in the South American selva.

The epiphytes do not obtain food from the trees, lianes or shrubs to which they are attached. How then can they live? The answer is that they develop in small cracks and hollows in trunks and branches, where minute quantities of *humus* can collect and provide them with food. This humus consists chiefly of the decayed remnants of other plants. A good water supply for the epiphytes comes from the abundant, all-year rainfall. Many of them are specially adapted to store water, and some even send down aerial roots which reach the soil and there obtain moisture and food. They do not all live in the same sort of environment: for example, some grow on rough barks, others on smooth barks. As you can see in the picture, the epiphyte there has spread a considerable distance along the liane. Sometimes an epiphyte may completely cover the trunk and lower branches of its support.

The picture also illustrates how the stream has influenced the adjoining forest. Along its banks there is so much more soil moisture and sunlight than in the depths of the forest that a denser undergrowth has developed. Notice the typical tall, slender tree on the right and the tangled mass of plants beneath it. Sometimes the trees and other plants on the two banks meet across the stream, leaving it to flow through a tunnel of living vegetation.

ANSWER THESE QUESTIONS

1 What is an epiphyte? Where does it live? How does it obtain food?
2 Why do you think the European woman in the picture is exploring by canoe?

6 A forest clearing: on the banks of the Amazon, Brazil

Most of the people of the Amazon forest are spread out thinly along the main rivers and streams. They live in small settlements, like this one in the picture, which they have established in forest clearings. This one is situated on the banks of the Amazon, in the state of Pará. The man in the canoe is the owner of the hut. He is one of the thousands of *caboclos*, or peasants, part European and part Indian, who pass lonely lives in such settlements. There are no roads or tracks through the forest to other settlements, and the canoe provides his only means of transport.

Note the type of forest that backs on to the *caboclo's* smallholding. You can pick out the different 'layers' of vegetation, from the very tall, slender trees down to the lowest shrubs, forming what appears from the river to be a solid green wall of vegetation. Having cut down the trees and burned the undergrowth, the *caboclo* built his home and began to cultivate the soil. The plants with large leaves (left) are bananas, and he also grows *manioc*, a starchy food plant, and beans. He has no agricultural implements: when he plants seeds, he simply presses them into the soil—usually with his foot. He catches fish in the river, which also provides him with his only water supply.

His hut is made of wooden boards and is thatched with palm leaves, and has been built on piles to raise it above the seasonal flood level. At some settlements there are twenty or thirty huts like this one, standing along the river bank. Each one has a landing stage of some kind and a canoe. At some settlements there is a longer wooden building called a *barracão* or trading post, with a larger landing stage. From time to time, say once a fortnight, the *caboclo* paddles his canoe to the *barracão* to sell his surplus manioc flour, or any Brazil nuts, *guaraná* seeds, or other forest produce that he has collected. He buys there canned foods, salt, cloth, and other goods, which have been brought to the *barracão* by river steamer. If he wishes, he can obtain goods on credit—with the result that he is almost always in debt to the trader!

ANSWER THESE QUESTIONS

1 What are the meanings of the Brazilian (Portuguese) words: *caboclo, barracão*?
2 Why are the landing stage and the canoe such important parts of small settlements like the one in the picture?

6

7 On the coast: a mangrove swamp, Nigeria

Along the coastal fringes of the three main equatorial forest regions there are strips of a different type of vegetation known as *mangrove swamp*. The picture shows part of the mangrove swamp in the Niger delta, just south-west of Port Harcourt, where the trees and shrubs are growing in tidal water. There are other stretches of mangrove swamp to the west, and southwards along the coasts of Cameroon, Gabon and Congo (Kinshasa). In South America they occur on the coast near the Amazon mouth, and in Asia on the coasts of Malaya, Thailand and elsewhere. They also occur on other tropical coasts, but they are most luxuriant on the edge of the equatorial forest.

As you can see in the picture, the mangrove swamp is difficult to penetrate. The men, who are carrying boxes of dynamite for use in oil prospecting, have hacked a path through this dense tangle of vegetation, which consists mostly of the tall arched roots of mangrove trees. A mass of roots and other vegetation like this is often termed a mangrove swamp forest. The long spreading roots help to anchor the mangroves in the shifting mud, and at the same time they support the trunks of the trees above water level, even at high tide. The swamp forest varies in height from about 6 feet to 100 feet or more, and the largest mangroves have enormous prop roots as thick as a man's body (*see* No. 8). There are many species of evergreen trees and shrubs besides the mangroves, and the type of vegetation in any part of the swamp forest depends on its location. Nearest the sea are plants which can flourish in salt water (like those in the picture), and behind these there may be others growing in a freshwater swamp, beyond the reach of the tides. On the landward side the different zones of swamp gradually merge into the true equatorial forest.

The close tangle of vegetation in the mangrove swamp causes a great deal of sediment to be deposited round the roots. In time so much sediment collects that the ground level rises above the water, and the mangroves then spread seawards. Thus the mangrove swamp may play an important part in reclamation of land from the sea. The mangrove trees themselves have some commercial value: their hard, durable timber is used for building and for firewood, and the bark for tanning.

ANSWER THESE QUESTIONS

1 What are the uses to the mangrove of its tall, arched roots?
2 How may a mangrove swamp play a part in reclaiming land from the sea?

8 Forest and waterway: a creek in the Niger delta, Nigeria

How would you deduce that this scene is near a coastal *mangrove swamp* (No. 7)? The clue is the great mangrove tree on the extreme right of the picture, with gigantic prop roots lifting its trunk high above the water. This is one of the numerous creeks, which link the channels or *distributaries* of the River Niger and create a complicated network of waterways, It is well within the mangrove swamp belt of the Niger delta but, as you see, this section of the bank has been cleared and settled. Besides the mangroves, there are coconut palms standing near the water's edge. With a magnifying glass you may be able to see the coconuts on some of the palms. Just beyond the coconut palms on the left and right of the picture are several banana plants—about ten feet high, with long, broad leaves (*see* No. 24). The Ibo people of this area grow both coconuts and bananas for food, as well as *yams*, and *cassava* (manioc). Their most important source of weath is the oil palm (*see* No. 17).

Generally speaking, the mangrove swamp belt is sparsely populated. The chief settlements are the ports which serve the equatorial forest zone, the largest being Port Harcourt, on the east side of the delta. Smaller settlements are scattered along the distributaries and creeks, like the one in the picture: you can just see the roofs of the huts through the trees (left). The huts are similar to the Amazon dwelling of No. 6. They are oblong, their walls are made of upright boards, and they are covered with an overhanging thatch of palm leaves. Here and there huts have been built on piles above the water. In these small villages all building materials, timber, palm leaves and lianes (dried and made into rope), are obtained from the forest.

The villager's means of transport, the canoe, is also derived from the forest, having been carved almost entirely out of a single tree trunk. Notice how the man on the left is propelling his canoe. You can perhaps see the wooden paddle, shaped rather like a large shovel, more clearly in the hands of the man in the background (right). Canoes are used extensively for local trade. River steamers call at the delta ports and serve the lower valley of the Niger and its tributary, the Benue.

ANSWER THESE QUESTIONS

1 Which trees and plants in the picture can you identify? Which of them provide food for the people?
2 How do the people make use of the forest for (a) building their homes, (b) making their canoes?

8

9 Aborigines of the forest: African pygmies hunting game

This picture was taken in the Ituri forest in the extreme north-east of Congo (Kinshasa), the former Belgian Congo—near the borders of Uganda and the Sudan. Like the West African forest of No. 1, it contains many trees about 120 feet high and others 60 to 80 feet high, and is dense: from the road it appears to be almost impenetrable. If you look closely at the picture, you will see how lianes have twined themselves round the trees. This is one of the principal homes of the African *pygmies*: people of small stature, only 4 feet to 4 feet 6 inches tall, with brown skins and broad noses, who live in the depths of the equatorial forest. The three men climbing the tree in the foreground are pygmies. It is early morning and they are setting out in search of game. Hunting the animals of the forest for food is an important part of the pygmy way of life. Among the commoner animals are the okapi and various kinds of antelopes and monkeys.

The grown-up men are the only people who hunt, and they work together as a group. When they have found where the animals are, the pygmies either wait in the trees for them to approach or attract them by imitating their cries. Some pygmies catch game in large nets, but these members of the Efe tribe hunt with bows and poisoned arrows. After the hunt they carry the game back to their camp and divide it between the families, according to their needs. Then they cook and eat the meat, along with the berries, fruits, nuts, roots and other plant foods that the women have gathered. The edible plants of the forest ripen at different times of the year, so that pygmies can always find something to gather and eat.

You will have noted from the picture how easily the pygmies climb the tall, slender trees, showing how much at home they are in the forest. They and their ancestors have lived here, hunting and gathering, for thousands of years. They are very probably the *aborigines*, or original inhabitants, of the equatorial forest. They are sometimes known as *negrillos*—a Spanish name meaning 'little Negroes'. As you will see later (No. 12), there are also pygmies in the equatorial forests of south-east Asia.

ANSWER THESE QUESTIONS

1 How would you describe the pygmies or negrillos of the Ituri forest?
2 What are the two ways in which the pygmies hunt game? What other kinds of food can they obtain from the forest?

9

Living in the forest: a pygmy building a home

Among the pygmies of the Ituri forest it is the women who build the homes. You can see in the picture how the pygmies have cleared a patch of forest for their camp, and a woman has started to build. They have chosen a spot near a stream, so that fresh water is always at hand. The woman has fixed a number of saplings in the ground, bending them over in a half circle to form a framework, and now she is making the 'roof' by laying plantain leaves over them. The hut will be simply a tiny shelter, rather like a beehive in shape, with sufficient leaves on top to protect the occupants from the heavy tropical rains. Dwellings are not needed for warmth, for the air temperature in the forest is always high, even at night. Eventually there will be a small cluster of these huts in the clearing, each one belonging to a family. Not far away the pygmies clear another patch of forest to serve as a playground for their children. On a hunting expedition the men of the camp work together (*see* No. 9): this co-operation helps to protect everyone, for a family on its own in the forest might not survive. When game and plant foods become scarce, the pygmies move to another part of the forest and build a new camp: they are *nomads*, or wanderers.

Some bands of pygmies, especially those who live near a Negro village, build larger and less primitive dwellings, and in time imitate their neighbours. Their huts are oblong, the walls are strongly made of upright sticks plastered with mud, and ridged roofs are thatched with leaves. Contact with the Negroes also brings them a more varied diet: when they have surplus game, or wild honey which they gather in the forest, they exchange these foods for the cassava (manioc) and plantains that are cultivated by the Negroes. But they seldom want to leave the forest, which provides them with food and shelter and is, as they say, their 'father and mother'. They are a timid people, shy of strangers and suspicious of the world outside the forest. Their Negro neighbours, on the other hand, generally dislike the dark, mysterious forest, and are only too willing to leave it to the pygmies.

ANSWER THESE QUESTIONS

1 How do the pygmies choose a site for their camp? How is the woman in the picture building her hut?

2 Why do you think the pygmies look upon the forest as their 'father and mother'? Why do they seldom move far from the forest?

Communal forest home: a longhouse in Sarawak

The children in the picture are looking towards their village home. They live in Sarawak and are Sea Dayaks or Ibans—one of the most important peoples in the great island of Borneo. If you consult an atlas map, you will see that the equator passes through Borneo: most of the island is covered with tropical rain forest. The children's home has been built in a large clearing: notice the dense forest in the background. It accommodates many families under the one roof and is known as a *longhouse*. As in other equatorial forest regions, the abundant rainfall feeds a large number of rivers and streams, and the longhouse is always built near one of them. Each day the women carry water from the river to the longhouse in large bamboo containers, and the river is where everyone does their washing and cleaning. The river is also the only means of communication, and the people travel by dugout canoe.

Look at the left-hand end of the longhouse, where an Iban man is standing on a platform near the entrance. This shows how the whole building is raised on piles which the Ibans have cut from the strong hardwood timber of the forest. When the children return home, they will have to climb to the platform by a notched tree trunk which serves as a ladder. The floor and walls of the longhouse are made of wood, and the overhanging roof consists of a thatch of overlapping palm leaves fixed to wooden rods and is proof against the frequent heavy downpours. Sometimes the roof is made of shingles, or wooden tiles. As you can see, sections of the roof can be raised to admit air and light. A corridor about half the width of the longhouse extends from end to end, like an indoor street, and alongside it are the living rooms, one to each family. In parts which require extra strength, such as the supporting piles and the ridge-pole of the roof, the Ibans use *ironwood*, a common tree which is well known for its toughness. They often use a type of *liane* called *rattan* (see No. 4) for fastening together the poles of the longhouse. They do not look on their longhouse as a permanent home: after some years they may pull it down, move elsewhere, and build another in a new forest clearing.

ANSWER THESE QUESTIONS

1 How would you describe an Iban longhouse? Where is it always built?
2 For what purpose do the Ibans use ironwood and rattan in building their longhouse?

12 *In the Malayan forest: Senoi with blowguns*

This picture, like No. 11, was taken in the equatorial forest zone of south-east Asia—in the interior of northern Malaya. Dense evergreen rain forest still covers the greater part of Malaya (*see* No. 13), and the area shown here has been cleared for human settlement. The two men belong to the Senoi, or Sakai, one of the aboriginal peoples of Malaya, and are engaged in hunting forest animals. Each man is holding a blowgun about eight feet long, which is the traditional hunting weapon and is made by boring a hole through a narrow bamboo. The dart that they shoot from the blowgun is made from the rib of a palm leaf, and is tipped with the poisonous sap or *latex* from the *upas* tree. A bamboo quiver full of darts is fastened to each hunter's belt.

Besides hunting game the Senoi grow food crops. When they clear a section of forest, they cut down the trees and shrubs, wait till they are dry and then burn them. The wood ash is washed into the soil by the rain and fertilises it. Now the Senoi plant small patches of land with such crops as *padi* (rice), cassava, and bananas: there is a banana tree with fruit on the extreme left of the picture. After one or two years the soil loses much of its fertility, and the Senoi abandon their tiny fields, clear another area of forest, and sow food crops there—a system of agriculture known as *shifting cultivation*. Some of the Senoi build new houses when they change plots, others stay in their houses and simply clear another patch for cultivation. In the background you can see the house belonging to the headman of the village. Again it illustrates how the people make use of the forest for home-buildings. It is raised several feet above the ground on wooden piles. The floor, rafters, and most of the other timber work is made of bamboo and the walls and thatched roof of interwoven palm leaves.

The Senoi are the most numerous of the Malayan *aborigines*. Another aboriginal people called the Semang do not cultivate the soil but live entirely by hunting and gathering in the forest, like the African pygmies (No. 9). They are short and rather dark-skinned and are known as *negritos* (another name for 'little Negroes').

ANSWER THESE QUESTIONS

1 How does the way of life of the Senoi (a) resemble, (b) differ from that of the African pygmies (No. 9)?
2 What is shifting cultivation?

13 *Effects of shifting cultivation: secondary forest in Malaya*

How does shifting cultivation affect the forest? What happens to the cultivated plots when they are abandoned by their owners? In this picture you see two men with their blowguns (the same two as in No. 12). They are walking through a patch of forest which the Senoi cleared, planted with crops, and then abandoned. It is now covered with a tangled mass of plants which, as they grow, will become more and more difficult to penetrate: this is termed *secondary forest*. The tallest trees here are only about 30 feet: the original or *primary forest*, in the background, is higher and less dense.

The primary forest in Malaya is much like that in other equatorial forest regions of the world. It has a great number of different species, as many as a hundred in an acre, including shrubs, lianes and epiphytes as well as trees. The trunks of the trees are tall and straight, and carry branches only near the top, where they form an almost continuous canopy. Some of them have buttresses which give extra support to their shallow roots. In the secondary forest there are also numerous species, as you can see in the picture, with many herbs, creepers and climbers, and trees that are not normally found in the primary forest. Among the tangle of plants you may be able to see a coarse grass known as *lalang*, which occupies a great deal of the secondary forest area. After some time, probably about ten years, the Senoi may return to this area, clear it again by burning, and grow crops. *Lalang* grass survives fire better than most plants, and so often predominates in secondary forest which has been repeatedly cleared for cultivation by man. If the land is left undisturbed, however, the primary forest will gradually return and replace the secondary—but the change would take centuries.

There are other causes for the change from primary to secondary forest. If a plantation (*see* No. 18) is abandoned, for example, the change will be similar. Very occasionally a natural fire, or in some areas a hurricane, may destroy the primary forest and bring about the change. Nearly always, however, man is responsible for the production of secondary forest.

ANSWER THESE QUESTIONS

1 What are the main differences between the primary forest and the secondary forest? What are the chief causes of the change from one to the other?

2 Why does *lalang* grass occupy a large part of the secondary forest?

14 Routes through the forest: road-making in Ghana

As previous pictures have shown, the equatorial forest is one of the most difficult regions in the world through which to travel. The actual construction of routes through the forest is still more difficult, and roads and railways are widely spaced or even over vast areas non-existent. To some extent great rivers such as the Amazon and the Congo and their tributaries serve as highways of trade. In districts away from the navigable rivers, like the one in the picture, in the rain forest of Ghana, *human porterage* has long been the normal method of transport. Goods are carried by men and women, often on the head, along forest paths. Sometimes the journeys are considerable, for many forest dwellers still live several days' walk from a road or a railway. Animal transport is ruled out because of the *tsetse fly*: an insect, common in the African rain forest, which spreads a fatal disease called *trypanosomiasis* among domestic animals.

The men in the picture are clearing a way through the forest in preparation for the making of a road. They are voluntary workers from a nearby village and have brought their own picks, shovels and knives. Already they have felled the trees and removed much of the undergrowth and are burning this vegetation (background). The man in the foreground is using his machete to cut away the remaining branches of a tree. Later a bulldozer will be used to finish the clearing process and level the track. Because the road will not be of major importance, it will have a dirt surface, like most of those in the forest region. Road-building materials are scarce, and only trunk roads and roads around large towns are bitumen surfaced. Maintenance as well as construction is both difficult and expensive, largely because of the climate. Violent downpours create ruts and potholes and may even wash away part of a road. A large tree, uprooted in a storm, may block a road for days.

In the past, roads were often made simply as offshoots to waterways or railways—or to serve particular mines or plantations. Poor communications have long retarded the economic development of the region. Roads are cheaper to construct and maintain than railways, and during recent years great efforts have been made in West Africa to provide a good system of all-weather roads.

ANSWER THESE QUESTIONS

1 Why are animals not used for transport in the African rain forest?

2 What are the chief difficulties in building and maintaining roads in the equatorial forest?

14

PART TWO: THE RESOURCES

15 *Timber from the forest: felling a tree in Ghana*

The equatorial forests occupy a large fraction of the total forest area of the world, but they contribute a very small part of the wood products that the world requires. You have already considered some of the reasons for this. One of their chief disadvantages from the point of view of the lumberman, for example, is the fact that the useful trees are so widely scattered. If he is seeking a particular type of tree, he will not discover large stands of the species, as he would, for instance, in the northern coniferous forests. A valuable and magnificent specimen like the one in the picture is surrounded by dozens of species of little or no value. Notice how close the trees are to the one being felled and how dense the undergrowth is, adding to the difficulties of the lumbermen. As you see, they have built themselves a platform on which to stand while they swing their axes. It raises them above the projecting buttresses of the tree and the undergrowth.

The different kinds of timber which come from the world's forests are classified as either softwood or hardwood. Softwoods are obtained from the coniferous forests, hardwoods either from the temperate broad-leaved forests or from the tropical rain forests: the wood from the tree in the picture would therefore be called a *tropical hardwood*. It is a type of mahogany, and it grows in the three main regions of equatorial forest. Mahogony is highly prized, especially for the making of furniture, veneers, etc., because of its attractive reddish-brown colour, and because it is hard and durable and takes a high polish. There are many different species of trees that yield wood known as mahogany. The one in the picture, which grows in Nigeria and the Ivory Coast as well as Ghana, would be sold as African mahogany. So, too, would the timber from a number of similar West African species.

Timber of this kind is an important export from Ghana, in recent years only second in value to cacao, another product of the equatorial forest region. Tropical hardwoods are also significant exports from Nigeria, Ivory Coast and Cameroon. In south-east Asia the Philippines export large quantities of hardwood timber, often classified as Philippine mahogany, and also rattans, bamboo, and other products of their extensive forests.

ANSWER THESE QUESTIONS

1 What are the difficulties of lumbering in the equatorial forest?
2 Why is mahogony such a highly prized timber?

16 *Timber transportation: floating logs at Sapele, Nigeria*

The most valuable timber trees, like the gigantic specimen you saw in No. 15, tower high above the main storeys of the forest. Their great size adds to the difficulties of felling and transportation. When the lumbermen have felled a tree, they strip off its branches and cut it into logs of similar length to those you see in the picture. They also remove the bark: you can see a small section of bark remaining on one of the logs. With the construction of more roads in West Africa during recent years, increasing quantities of logs are being transported by lorry for at least part of the journey to the coast. Usually the logs are so heavy and bulky that a lorry can carry only two or three in each load.

Much of the timber cut in the West African forest, however, is floated down the rivers. Here in Nigeria the logs are made up into rafts, three hundred being the maximum number permitted in each one, and these are then towed by tugs to the port. As you see, wire ropes passing through rings fixed to the logs hold them together. The two men on the right, who have come here by dugout canoe, are checking the logs, while the man on the left is using his long pole to move the logs about. In the background there are more logs from the same raft. Notice how dense the vegetation is along the banks of the river. Most of the timber exported from Nigeria comes from the area north and north-west of the timber port of Sapele, in the Western Region. It is shipped mainly as logs, but a processing industry has also developed at Sapele and elsewhere: sawmills export sawn timber (planks), and factories produce plywood and veneers.

In addition to the increased overseas demand for West African timber, requirements in the region itself are also high. Much is needed for building, and, in view of the scarcity of coal, for fuel. There are more than three hundred timber-producing species in Ghana alone, some of which are put to special uses because of their individual qualities. The *wawa*, for instance, is lighter in weight and softer than most timbers from the equatorial forest, and so is used in making the dugout canoes that are such an important means of transport in the region.

ANSWER THESE QUESTIONS

1 How is timber floated down the rivers in Nigeria? From which port is most of it exported?
2 Why is the wood of the *wawa* used in making dugout canoes?

17 *Food from the forest: climbing an oil palm in Nigeria*

Some trees are valuable for products other than timber. The picture shows one of them: the oil palm, which is useful chiefly because it yeilds two kinds of vegetable oil. It is a native of the equatorial forest zone of West Africa, and is especially common in the area around the lower River Niger, in southern Nigeria. The country which became Nigeria, in fact, was once called the Oil Rivers Protectorate, because of its association with the main product of the tree.

As you see in the picture, when the oil palm has to compete for sunlight and air with a dense mass of other trees, it grows into a tall, slender tree. Sometimes it reaches a height of 60 feet. Like other palms it has no branches, but a number of long feathery leaves or fronds spreading out from the top. Leaves of nearby less lofty oil palms are also visible in the picture. The man who is climbing the palm is going to cut down the fruit, which hangs in bunches at the top of the trunk between the leaves. As you see, he is secured by a rope looped round his waist and the trunk of the palm, and in his right hand he carries a machete. Like every other young man in the district, he learned to climb the oil palms when he was a boy. It is a dangerous occupation: in the past climbers have injured themselves severely when they have accidentally cut through the safety rope and fallen to the ground. For this reason many Africans nowadays cut down the fruit with a curved knife fixed to the end of a long bamboo pole (*see* No. 18).

The villagers use other parts of the palm besides the oil from the fruit, which is an important food. They use the leaves for thatching their houses and for making baskets and brooms. Fibre left after the oil has been squeezed out of the fruit and shells from the nuts inside the fruit make good fuel. Some Africans also tap the trunks of wild oil palms and make the liquid they obtain into palm wine. The tree is usually considered too valuable to be felled, but when this is necessary the trunk and the central ribs of the leaves are used in building.

ANSWER THESE QUESTIONS

1 Why was the Oil Rivers Protectorate so called? Which part of modern Nigeria did it occupy?

2 What parts of the oil palm do the people use, and for what purposes?

18 Oil palm plantation: harvesting the fruit

In this picture you see oil palms on a Nigerian *plantation*: an estate where a single *cash crop* is grown. A cash crop is one produced for sale and not for consumption by the grower. There are several advantages in producing oil from these cultivated palms rather than from the wild palms. First, all the palms are together and are easily reached: wild palms are often scattered and difficult to find. Second, these palms begin to fruit only four years after being planted: the wild palm does not fruit for twelve years or more. Third, the cultivated palm gives much more oil than the wild palm. The picture illustrates yet another advantage. When the palms were planted, a distance of about 30 feet was left between the rows and almost as much between the individual palms. Workers have also cleared the undergrowth around each palm. This extra space has caused the palms to grow much thicker and also shorter than the wild palms: they can be harvested by hand for about eight years after beginning to fruit, whereas the wild palms are so tall that they have to be climbed as soon as they start to fruit. The worker in the picture has just cut down the first bunch of fruit from the palm, using the curved knife on the pole. You can see another bunch between two of the leaves (upper left).

There are as many as six bunches on the palm, each one containing several hundred fruits. The worker is putting the bunches of fruit, each of which weighs 30 lb. or more, in the baskets. These are collected by lorry and taken to the mill. The fruit is reddish-yellow and, as you see, about the size of a plum. Inside its skin is the pulp, or *pericarp*, which contains the valuable palm oil, and inside this is a nut containing a kernel, from which a second kind of oil is obtained. Because of careful, scientific methods of cultivation, the fruit grown on the plantations has a thicker pericarp than the wild fruit and therefore yields more oil. Modern machinery used on the plantations also extracts a higher proportion of oil from the fruit than the more primitive equipment of the villager. Palm oil obtained from the wild palms, however, still forms an important part of the African's diet in the forest region.

ANSWER THESE QUESTIONS

1 What are the advantages of producing palm oil from the cultivated palms (in a plantation) rather than from wild palms?

2 What are the two kinds of oil obtained from the oil palm?

19 *The wild rubber tree: tapping in the Amazon basin*

This photograph has historical as well as geographical interest, for it was taken in the Amazon forest early this century. It shows the tree which has become the source of nearly all the world's supply of natural rubber: a tree which is native to the Amazon basin and has the scientific name *Hevea brasiliensis*. Notice again the close tangle of trees, shrubs, and lianes that surround it. In the wild state the rubber tree may grow to a height of over 100 feet, like the one in the picture, far taller and thicker than the plantation tree (*see* No. 21).

The inner bark of the rubber tree contains a milky liquid called *latex*, from which rubber is produced. Do you see the long V-shaped white streaks on the tree in the picture? These are the cuts that the rubber gatherer (left) has made in the outer bark of the tree in order to free the latex. The latex has drained down to the central vertical cut and from this has dripped into the container at the foot of the tree. As you see, the gatherer has made two new cuts with the help of a knife on the end of a long stick. He will make similar cuts in a large number of other trees scattered about the forest, as many as two hundred altogether. When the flow of latex has stopped, he will collect the liquid from these trees, and take it away to convert it into solid rubber. He does this by dipping a wooden pole in the latex and holding it in the smoke from a slowly burning fire. The method is still in use in the Amazon forest today.

In the nineteenth century the world's rubber was produced by these methods in the Amazon basin and exported from Belém. As the demand increased, thousands of workers were settled along the river to collect rubber, and Indians too were recruited. You can imagine from the picture their difficulties in cutting paths through the forest, finding the scattered rubber trees, and continually striving to produce more and more rubber. It was not surprising that their methods were crude and careless, that they sometimes damaged and even killed the trees. By the time this picture was taken, plantations had been established in south-east Asia, and the Amazon basin had lost its place as the world's main rubber-producing area.

ANSWER THESE QUESTIONS

1 What part of the rubber tree contains the latex? How does the gatherer in the Amazon forest convert it into solid rubber?

2 How would you describe the geographical position of Belém? (Use your atlas.)

20 *Plantation rubber: bud-grafting in Malaya*

When the early rubber plantations were planned, the first problem was to obtain some seeds of *Hevea brasiliensis*. A young Englishman named Wickham (later Sir Henry Wickham), who had already explored the Amazon forests, undertook the task. With the help of Indians he collected 70,000 seeds, packed them, and sent them to Kew Gardens in London. Many of the seeds were planted in the hothouses there, and about 2,000 young plants from these seeds were then despatched to Ceylon and Malaya. In those countries, in a similar climate to that of the Amazon forest, the seedlings flourished and plantations were established.

The saplings in the picture are young rubber trees growing on a plantation in Malaya. Single seeds are first sown in baskets of soil, and the seedlings are carefully tended until they are six to nine weeks old. Workers then transplant the seedlings into prepared ground, usually sowing a *cover crop* in alternate rows with them. A cover crop is one which helps to hold the soil together and prevent it from being washed away by the violent tropical rains (*soil erosion*). When the young trees are nine months old they are ready for *bud-grafting*, the process which the Indian worker in the picture is carrying out. He has cut away a flap of bark from the tree and is holding this with his left hand. In his right hand he has a thin strip of wood containing a bud, cut from a special high-yielding tree—one which produces a large quantity of latex. He is inserting the bud wood under the flap, which he will then replace and bind up. In a few weeks' time, when a young shoot grows from here, he will cut off the stem of the original tree. The new shoot will then grow into a high-yielding rubber tree.

Careful seed selection and the practice of bud-grafting have enormously raised the rubber output of the Malayan plantations. When bud-grafting experiments were first made, the best yield that the planters could expect was about 300 lb. of rubber per acre per year. Today they are obtaining annual yields of 2,000 lb. or more per acre. Research and the use of new methods have also helped the rubber planters in other ways. These include the study of soils, the application of fertilisers, and the control of the pests and diseases which attack the rubber tree.

ANSWER THESE QUESTIONS

1 Sir Henry Wickham was called 'the father of plantation rubber'. Why?
2 What is (a) a cover crop, (b) bud-grafting?

21 *Plantation rubber: tapping the trees*

The picture shows rubber trees on a modern Malayan plantation, and you will notice several differences between this scene and the one in No. 19. First, when the plantation was established, the vegetation of the original rain forest was completely cleared and burned. Second, the rubber trees are several feet apart in neat rows, with a greater distance between the rows. Third, as the Indian woman demonstrates, the workers use a more efficient method of tapping the trees. After the trees had been planted here, they were not ready for tapping until they were five or six years old—but they will go on producing *latex* for thirty years or more. They are not allowed to grow to the enormous size of the wild tree in No. 19.

You can see the panel of bark that the worker has cut away on each of the trees—a panel which slopes gently downwards and extends halfway round the trunk. She is now cutting away a thin strip of bark at the bottom of the panel, using a tapping knife, which has a wooden handle and a long blade curved at the cutting end. She began work soon after dawn and she will have to stop about midday. Heavy rain often falls in the afternoon in this equatorial region and would spoil the latex, so all the tapping has to be done in the morning. When the woman has made the cut, the latex will flow gently along the groove and drip from a spout into a cup that is wired to the trunk. You can see the latex in the cups on trees that she has already visited. Later in the morning she will collect the latex from the 300 to 400 trees she has visited and take it to the plantation factory. She allows these trees to recover from the cuts by tapping them on alternate days with other lines of trees, In three to four years she will have finished cutting the panel, and she will then start cutting on the other side of the trunk. When that panel is completed, six to eight years from the start of cutting, the bark on the near side will have been renewed. Then the woman—or other workers —will be able to begin tapping the tree on the first panel again.

ANSWER THESE QUESTIONS

1 What are the differences between this scene on a rubber plantation and that of No. 19?
2 Why does the woman in the picture work on the plantation only in the morning? How does she obtain the latex from the trees?

22 *The cacao tree: harvesting on a Nigerian farm*

The cacao tree, illustrated in the picture, is the source of our cocoa and chocolate. Its scientific name is *Theobroma cacao*, which means 'cacao, food of the gods'. It is a native of the tropical rain forests of Central and South America, but the cultivated tree has become more important in the corresponding region of West Africa, especially in Ghana and Nigeria. The picture shows a Nigerian farmer harvesting his crop. It is more correct to term the cacao-producing plots farms rather than plantations, for each farmer usually owns only three or four acres of land.

You may have noticed in the picture an unusual feature of the cacao tree: its flowers and fruits are not attached to twigs but to the trunk and branches. If you look carefully you can see one of the small pink flowers growing from the trunk (top centre). Just below it is a tiny pod, which has developed from another flower. During the year the tree will bear about 6,000 blossoms, but only about 25 to 30 of these will become fully grown pods (fruits). Notice, too, that the pods vary greatly in size. In the equatorial forest region the growth of vegetation is continuous, so that blossoms, small pods and large pods may be seen on a tree at the same time. At first the pods are green, but as they grow they change to golden yellow and even purple when they are ripe. They are ribbed and they grow to about eight inches in length. The farmer in the picture is cutting down only the fully grown pods with his cutlass.

In starting to grow cacao trees the West African farmer often sows the seeds first in a nursery bed, and then transplants the seedlings when they are about a year old. When he clears the original forest for his plot, he may leave some of the taller trees to provide shade. He removes and burns the rest of the vegetation and hoes in the ashes to make the soil more fertile. The trees begin to bear fruit in four or five years, and will continue to do so for twenty years or more. They will grow to about 40 feet in the wild state, but the farmer usually prunes them to about half this height in order to make harvesting easier.

ANSWER THESE QUESTIONS

1 What is unusual about the flowers and fruits of the cacao tree?
2 Why may blossoms and pods of different sizes be seen on the cacao tree at the same time?

22

23 *The cacao beans: on a farm in Ghana*

Although the growth of the cacao trees and their fruits is continuous, there are two main harvesting seasons in West Africa. This farmer in Ghana gathers his principal crop from October to December, and a second smaller crop from March to May. At harvest time he is helped by other members of his family. Some of them are helping him to cut down the cacao pods, put them into baskets and carry them on their heads to this spot among the trees. Several others here are sitting round the baskets of cacao pods. You can see two of them and also one of the baskets on the left. Each of them has a cutlass and is cutting open the pods. They scoop out the beans, or seeds, inside the pods and throw aside the husks, many of which you can see in the picture (centre right).

There are thirty or forty beans in each pod embedded in a white pulp, and the farmer has collected a heap of them with their pulp near his helpers. He has placed them on a layer of plantain leaves and is now covering them with more plantain leaves. He will leave the covered heap for several days, and during this time the pulp will ferment, turn liquid, and drain away. This fermentation process serves a double purpose: it gets rid of the unwanted pulp and it improves the quality and flavour of the beans, at the same time changing their colour from white to brown. Next the farmer spreads out the beans on long tables covered with mats in the open air, turning them over each day until they are all thoroughly and evenly dried by the sun. Finally the beans are put into sacks and transported to the coast for export. Strictly speaking, they should be called cocoa only when they have been processed in the factory.

Cacao is the chief cash crop in Ghana and in other parts of West Africa, but the farmers also cultivate *subsistence crops*: crops which they and their families consume. Among the commoner subsistence crops are bananas (or plantains) and yams, which the farmers often use as shade trees for the cacao seedlings. Yams provide a starchy food in their tubers—rather like potatoes.

ANSWER THESE QUESTIONS

1 When does this farmer in Ghana harvest his main cacao crops?
2 How does he prepare the beans for export?

24 *The banana plant: harvesting in Jamaica*

The banana is grown in all three major areas of the equatorial forest region. It is extensively cultivated as a subsistence crop: the ripe fruit contains a considerable amount of sugar and several vitamins. There are dozens of varieties of banana, including the plantains, which are scarcely ever seen outside the tropics. Plantains are starchy rather than sweet and are always cooked before being eaten. The banana is also grown as a cash crop on plantations. In temperate lands, where it is probably the most popular of tropical fruits, the best known variety has the scientific name *Musa sapientum*. This means 'fruit of the wise men', a name given to it because wise men in India are supposed to have long ago rested in its shade and eaten the fruit.

The banana plant requires high temperatures and an annual rainfall of 80 inches or so, well distributed throughout the year. On the north-east side of Jamaica, where the picture was taken, and where equatorial forest once covered the land, this abundant rainfall is brought by the north-east trade wind. This is where most of the banana plantations are situated. On the south side of the island, shielded by mountains from the rain-bearing trade wind, the rainfall decreases to about 30 inches annually. Here bananas have to be grown by *irrigation*: that is, by providing an artificial supply of water to make up for the insufficient rainfall.

You saw a banana plant with its fruit in No. 12. About a year after planting it reached a height of 15 to 30 feet and is surmounted by a number of large leaves, some of which you can see in the picture. Its flowers develop into a single bunch of fruit, arranged in clusters or 'hands'. The worker in the picture has pulled down the stem, has cut off the end, and is about to cut it again just above the fruit. When the plant is growing the stem bends right over, so that the bananas are pointing upwards. A bunch like the one here weighs 50 lb. or more, and makes the plant top-heavy and easily broken down by a strong wind. Jamaica and other islands in the Caribbean area are occasionally visited by a *hurricane* (a violent tropical storm), and when this occurs it causes enormous damage on the banana plantations.

ANSWER THESE QUESTIONS

1 What useful food substances does the banana contain? How does the plantain differ from it?

2 What is the rain-bearing wind of Jamaica? Why does the north side have a heavier rainfall than the south?

25 *Abacá or Manila hemp: a plantation in Sabah*

This picture was taken on a plantation in Sabah (formerly British North Borneo), now part of Malaysia, in the north-east of the great island of Borneo. Look at the leaves of the plants in the picture. Do they remind you of the leaves of plants that you have seen in previous pictures? They belong to the *abacá* plant, which is closely related to the banana and the plantain: its scientific name is *Musa textilis*—the common variety of banana, you remember, is *Musa sapientum*. Its leaves are similar to those of the banana and plantain but are narrower, and its fruits, while resembling small bananas, are uneatable. It is not cultivated for its fruits, but for the fibre contained in its stalks, which are clearly visible in the picture.

The abacá plant is grown from root stalks, or suckers, and about two years after planting it flowers and is ready for fibre production. As you see, it consists of a cluster of stalks, each one formed from overlapping leaf stems, with several long, overhanging leaves at the top. To obtain the fibre, the workers cut down the stalks near the ground and remove the leaves. Then they separate the leaf stems, scrape away pulp and other unwanted material, clean the fibre, and hang it on racks to dry and bleach in the sun. As you can judge from the height of the plants, the strips of fibre are about 8 to 12 feet in length. Abacá fibre, which is also known as *Manila hemp*, is very strong and durable and resists the action of salt water as well as fresh water, and so is useful in the manufacture of ships' ropes, etc. It is also made into various kinds of paper.

In Sabah the abacá plants suffer from a disease which spreads from wild bananas in the neighbourhood and may eventually kill them. The workers in the picture are spraying the plants with a chemical to protect them against this disease. In the Philippines the production of abacá fibre is much greater than in Sabah. The island of Luzon has the constant high temperatures, plentiful rainfall, and fertile soil which are needed for successful abacá cultivation, but the plantations there suffer severely from *typhoons*. These are the violent tropical storms of the China Seas, similar to the hurricanes which occasionally destroy the banana plantations in the West Indies (*see* No. 24).

ANSWER THESE QUESTIONS

1 How does the abacá plant differ from the banana and plantain?
2 What is the name of the tropical storms that sometimes damage the abacá plantations in the Philippines? What is the corresponding storm in the Caribbean area (No. 24)?

26 Pepper gardens: intensive cultivation in Sarawak

Much of the vast island of Borneo, including Sarawak, still consists of tropical rain forest. In the background of the picture, on the far side of the river, forest stretches to the distant horizon. Notice how dense the vegetation is along the opposite river bank, where trees and other plants have abundant sunlight and soil moisture. The land in the foreground, on the near side of the river, was long ago cleared of its original forest by the shifting cultivation of the inhabitants, with rice as the main crop. A *secondary forest* growth developed, consisting of coarse *lalang* grass and low bushes. Chinese farmers, one of whom you see in the picture (bottom right), have now cleared patches of this secondary forest for their pepper gardens. The river, on which you see a shallow-draught steamer, is the Rejang (Rajang), the main waterway of Sarawak. As in other equatorial forest regions, a river plays the chief role in the transport system: Sarawak has no railways and only a small road mileage.

The plots of land on which you can see neat rows of conical plants are the pepper gardens. These plants are often termed *vines* because they are climbers, and they are trained to grow up tall hardwood poles stuck in the ground. As you see, the plants in some of the gardens are at varying stages of growth. Some of them have only a clump of grass at the foot which shades the tender young pepper plant. The growers keep the plants to a height of 10 to 12 feet. They also keep the ground clear of weeds and frequently enrich the soil around the plants with fertiliser. In two or three years the plants start to bear fruit, and the growers and their families pick the small round berries when they have changed from green to red. They spread some of the berries on mats to dry in the sun: when the berries, now black, are ground, the product is called *black pepper*. The growers soak the best berries in water till the outer skins and pulp are removed and the seeds when dried become the more valuable *white pepper*. In cultivating their pepper gardens they put a great deal of capital and labour into a small area of land: a method of agriculture known as *intensive cultivation*.

ANSWER THESE QUESTIONS

1 The vegetation on some of the land here has changed three times. What have the changes been?
2 How do the Chinese farmers tend their pepper vines? What two kinds of pepper do they produce?

27 *Forest and padi fields: terrace cultivation in Java*

In this picture, as in No. 26, you can see land which is still occupied by the original forest adjoining land which was long ago cleared for cultivation. This is near Bandung, in western Java, the most important though not the largest island in Indonesia. Can you find any evidence to suggest that the vegetation in the background is equatorial forest? Look at the tall trees, mostly with straight trunks, but without branches and foliage below the crown. Notice how dense part of this forest is (upper left). Do you see the scattered banana plants with their large leaves? If you look closely, you may be able to see the bunch of fruit on one of them (lower left). This banana and the nearby palm now stand in *secondary forest*.

The small flat areas on the lower hill slopes are *padi* (*paddy*) or rice fields, which the Javanese peasants have cultivated for centuries by hard manual labour. They cut the tiny fields, which are no bigger than gardens, into the hill slopes in a series of steps or terraces, enclosing each one with a bank of earth. This method of agriculture, known as *terrace cultivation*, checks soil erosion, an ever-present danger when slopes are cultivated. It also allows control of the level of water in the fields: an important factor in rice cultivation, for the crop grows in standing water. The peasants first sow the rice in carefully prepared seed beds. Then they transplant the young plants into these fields, where the soil is covered with water which flows gently down from terrace to terrace. They maintain the depth of water according to the height of the growing rice, which you can see in the nearer fields in the picture, and drain away the water when the crop is ready for harvesting.

You will remember that some equatorial forest regions, especially in the Amazon basin, have a low *density of population* (number of people per square mile). In western Java, however, the soil is much more fertile than in other equatorial forest regions. In the course of centuries, too, the peasants have cleared much of the original forest, established terrace cultivation extensively, and have achieved high yields, often harvesting two rice crops in the year. Thus they have been able to maintain an exceptionally high density of population.

ANSWER THESE QUESTIONS

1 What is terrace cultivation?

2 Why is the density of population in western Java so much higher than in other parts of the equatorial forest zone?

28 Control of soil erosion: cassava cultivation in Togo

The men in the picture, which was taken in Togo, West Africa, are tilling the soil with an implement that is often called a hand plough. As you see, it is used like a hoe, and with similar implements is the traditional farming tool in tropical Africa. The crop for which the men are preparing the mounds of earth is cassava, sometimes known as manioc (*see* No. 6). This plant, a native of South America, provides one of the principal foods of the equatorial forest zone in all three major regions, taking the place of bread and potatoes in the diet. It gives a high yield and does not require specially fertile soils. The farmers grow cassava from cuttings, which they plant in mounds, as in the picture, or in the level ground, three or four feet apart. It has a slender stem and grows to a height of about nine feet. The food comes from its enlarged roots or tubers, which are peeled, washed and grated. Then the pulp is put in a bag and the liquid squeezed out, and the residue is sieved and slowly dried to form a meal, or flour.

Can you suggest why the men are going to plant the cassava in mounds? They are doing this to prevent soil erosion. In the equatorial forest zone rainfall is abundant, often violent, but the trees break its force, and their roots hold the soil and absorb much of the moisture: there is small danger of soil erosion. If the forest is cleared so that crops can be grown, however, a single torrential downpour may wash away the topsoil. These men are taking the precaution of breaking up the surface of the ground into mounds and hollows. Notice that they have also left some of the original trees so that the roots will bind together the soil particles. They are also going to plant maize in the hollows between the mounds so that it will act as a cover crop for the cassava (*see* No. 20). In some parts of West Africa the farmers divide the soil into small basins instead of mounds and hollows. Notice, too, the great quantity of weeds in the foreground. Although such weeds give an appearance of untidiness and neglect to many African farms, they do help to protect the farmer's land from soil erosion.

ANSWER THESE QUESTIONS

1 What part of the cassava plant is eaten and how it is prepared?
2 What is the great danger of clearing the equatorial forest in order to grow crops? How are the farmers in the picture taking precautions against this danger?

Do You Remember?

See if you remember the meaning of these terms—
then check by referring to the right pages

FURTHER WORK

1 Draw a map of North America and South America showing the equatorial forests (see end-paper A). Show also the Arctic Circle, Antarctic Circle, Tropic of Cancer, Tropic of Capricorn, Equator.

2 Describe a journey of exploration by canoe through the South American selva.

3 Draw diagrams to show the output of rubber in these countries: Malaya, Indonesia, Nigeria, Brazil (see FACTS AND FIGURES).

4 Write notes on the two great rivers of the equatorial forest zone, the Amazon and the Congo, mentioning chief tributaries, rapids and waterfalls, use as waterways, river ports. Illustrate your notes with sketch-maps of the two river basins.

5 Use reference books to find out facts about the animal life of the equatorial forests of South America, Central Africa, and South-east Asia. Condense the facts into a short written account for each region.

6 Make a list of the tropical hardwoods that are used in furniture making and illustrate your list with pictures of (a) the trees, (b) the cut timber.

7 Draw a map of Africa, Asia and Australia showing the equatorial forests (see end-paper B). Show also the Arctic Circle, Antarctic Circle, Tropic of Cancer, Tropic of Capricorn, Equator.

8 Compare the climate of Belém (Brazil) with that of Singapore (see FACTS AND FIGURES).

9 Draw diagrams to show the output of cocoa in these countries: Ghana, Nigeria, Brazil (see FACTS AND FIGURES).

10 Write a short account of the processes by which palm oil and palm kernels are used in the manufacture of margarine and soap.

11 Draw diagrams to show the output of palm oil and kernels in these countries: Nigeria, Congo (Kinshasa), Indonesia, Malaya (see FACTS AND FIGURES).

12 Find out how latex is converted into solid rubber on a modern Malayan plantation. Write a summary of the different processes.

13 Draw diagrams to show (a) the trunk and large branches of a cacao tree, with pods, (b) a pod in cross-section, with beans.

14 Find out what you can and write notes about the tsetse fly. Explain how it has prevented the use of horses and oxen as beasts of burden in the equatorial forest zone of Africa.

15 Collect pictures of the aboriginal peoples and their homes in the three great equatorial forest regions and classify them according to continents: South America, Africa, Asia.

16 Arrange the following products from the equatorial forest zone in three lists, (a) gathered, (b) cultivated, (c) gathered and cultivated: cassava (manioc), palm oil, Brazil nuts, abacá (Manila hemp), rattan, white pepper, bananas.

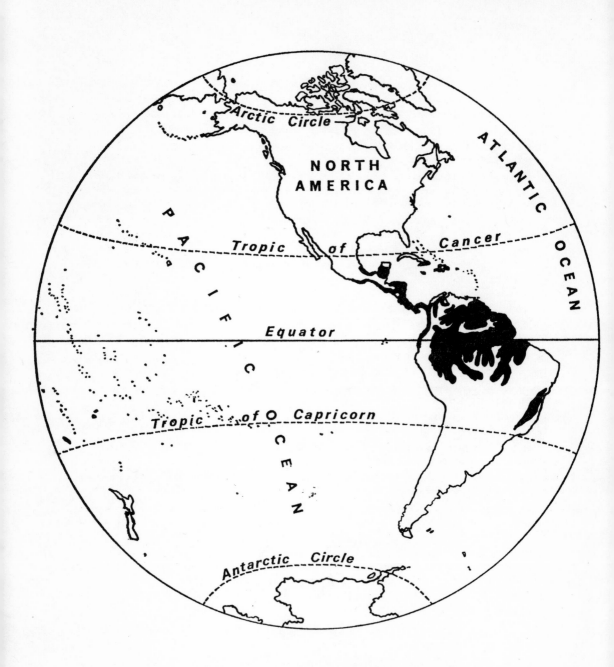

A. THE EQUATORIAL FORESTS OF
CENTRAL AND SOUTH AMERICA